Nellie's Trip Around the World

Published in the UK by Scholastic Education, 2023
Scholastic Distribution Centre, Bosworth Avenue, Tournament Fields, Warwick, CV34 6UQ
Scholastic Ireland, 89E Lagan Road, Dublin Industrial Estate, Glasnevin, Dublin, D11 HP5F

SCHOLASTIC and associated logos are trademarks and/or registered trademarks of Scholastic Inc.
www.scholastic.co.uk
© 2023 Scholastic
1 2 3 4 5 6 7 8 9   3 4 5 6 7 8 9 0 1 2

Printed by Ashford Colour Press
The book is made of materials from well-managed, FSC®-certified forests and other controlled sources.

A CIP catalogue record for this book is available from the British Library.
ISBN 978-0702-32115-3

All rights reserved. This book is sold subject to the condition that it shall not, by way of trade or otherwise, be lent, hired out or otherwise circulated in any form of binding or cover other than that in which it is published. No part of this publication may be reproduced, stored in a retrieval system, or transmitted in any form or by any other means (electronic, mechanical, photocopying, recording or otherwise) without prior written permission of Scholastic.

Every effort has been made to trace copyright holders for the works reproduced in this publication, and the publishers apologise for any inadvertent omissions.

Author
Alice Hemming

Editorial team
Rachel Morgan, Vicki Yates, Fiona Undrill, Jennie Clifford

Design team
Dipa Mistry, Andrea Lewis, We Are Grace

Illustrations
Carlo Molinari/Advocate Art

Help your child to read!

This book practises these letters and letter sounds.
Point and say the sounds with your child:

- or (as in 'work')
- oul (as in 'should')
- are (as in 'cared')
- ear (as in 'wear')
- ere (as in 'where')
- ture (as in 'adventure')
- a (as in 'called')
- a (as in 'was')
- wr (as in 'writer')
- st (as in 'listen')
- unstressed vowel sound at the end of a word (as in 'author')

Your child may need help to read these common tricky words:

who, to, many, people, said, the, two, of, were, do

Before reading
- Look at the cover picture and read the title together. Read the back cover blurb to your child.
- Ask your child: *Would you like to go on an adventure around the world?*
- Talk about the image in the magnifying glass.

During reading
- If your child gets stuck on a word, remind them to sound it out and then blend the sounds to read the word: w-or-l-d, world.
- If they are still stuck, show them how to read the word.
- Enjoy looking at the pictures together. Pause to talk about the information.

After reading
- Talk about the images on page 24. What can your child tell you about them?
- Ask your child: *Did you think Nellie would make it home in 80 days?*
- Discuss travelling with your child. Which countries would they like to visit? Would they rather travel by aeroplane or by ship and train, like the old days?

Nellie Bly was a writer and adventurer who lived in America over 100 years ago.

Nellie's real name was Elizabeth Cochran.

As a child, Elizabeth liked to wear pink and was called 'Pinky'.

Elizabeth loved school but when she was six, her father died, leaving her family poor.

At 15, she was too poor to finish school and had to work.

Many people back then said girls should stay indoors and not work. Elizabeth didn't listen!

She became a writer for a newspaper called the *New York World*. Using the writing name Nellie Bly, she wrote stories she cared about.

A French author wrote a book called *Around the World in 80 Days*. His main character finished the long trip in record time.

Nellie asked to try the same adventure.

Her boss wouldn't listen. He said no, that she would need protecting and would pack too much to wear.

With two days to prepare, Nellie had a hardwearing dress made.

In a small bag, she packed a change of outfit, underwear, writing equipment and cream for her skin.

Nellie sailed to London, then France, where she met the *80 Days* author.

As she travelled, there were setbacks but she enjoyed all the hustle and bustle of new places. She spent Christmas in China.

Her adventures interested people. The newspaper gave prizes for estimating her arrival time.

Another newspaper sent a reporter – Elizabeth Bisland – to race Nellie.

Nellie arrived back in New York where she discovered she'd set a world record of 72 days!

The other reporter arrived a few days later.

There were films, books and a play written about her adventures.

Talk about it!